AF433685

ELEMENTARY PARTICLES: THE BUILDING BLOCKS OF THE UNIVERSE

PHYSICS AND THE UNIVERSE CHILDREN'S PHYSICS BOOKS

Speedy Publishing LLC

40 E. Main St. #1156

Newark, DE 19711

www.speedypublishing.com

Copyright 2017

All Rights reserved. No part of this book may be reproduced or used in any way or form or by any means whether electronic or mechanical, this means that you cannot record or photocopy any material ideas or tips that are provided in this book

In this book, we're going to talk about the building blocks of the universe. So, let's get right to it!

The science behind the structure of all matter is still happening today. In numerous locations throughout the world, physicists work in linear accelerators to discover new properties of atomic and subatomic particles. Linear accelerators are devices that speed up particles using a series of electrical fields.

PROTOTYPE LINEAR ACCELERATOR

BOY USING MICROSCOPE OUTDOOR

HISTORY OF ATOMIC STRUCTURE

Everything you see around you is made up of atoms, but you can't see the atoms because they're too small. The typical size of an atom is 100 picometers. A picometer is one trillionth, written as $\frac{1}{1,000,000,000,000}$, of a meter. Atoms are so small that your body is made up of trillions of them.

It took a very long time for philosophers and scientists to understand the atom. In 450 BC the Greek philosopher, Democritus proposed a question. What would happen if you took an apple and divided into smaller and smaller pieces? He thought you would eventually get to a form of matter that couldn't be divided. He called this "uncuttable matter" *atomos* and this is where the term "atom" originates.

ATOM WITH ELECTRONS

JOHN DALTON

It was many centuries before the theories that Democritus had posed were brought back to the forefront again by the British chemist John Dalton. Around the year 1800, he developed a series of atomic theories and he conducted experiments to back up his claims. Many of his theories are still accepted today, but he thought that atoms were the smallest particles of matter, which wasn't correct.

In 1897, J.J. Thomson, a British physicist, discovered the electron. It was the first subatomic particle to be found. He thought that these negatively charged electrons were floating in a "sea" of matter that was positively charged.

In 1905, the famous physicist Albert Einstein published his important equation $E = mc^2$, which states the relationship between energy, matter, and the speed of light.

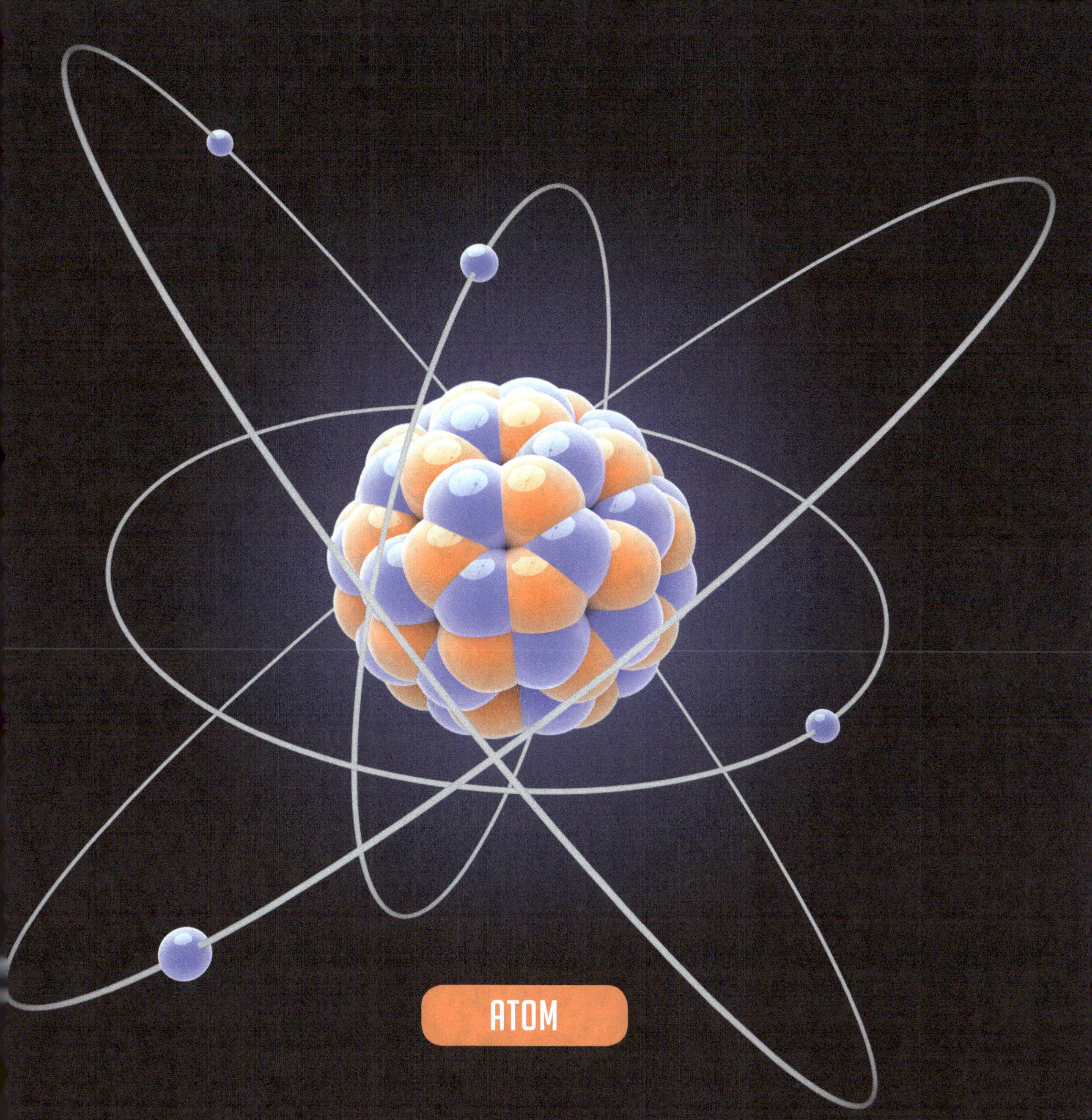

ATOM

ERNEST RUTHERFORD

Einstein's equation predicted that the splitting of the atom would unleash a huge amount of energy.

In 1911, Ernest Rutherford, a physicist from New Zealand, discovered the atom's nucleus. He later determined that the nucleus had protons that were positively charged and that electrons spun around this nucleus core.

In 1932, one of Rutherford's students, James Chadwick, discovered neutrons. Rutherford had predicted the existence of neutrons, but hadn't been able to find them.

Electrons, protons, and neutrons are the basic parts of an atom, but as scientists have started work with linear accelerators, many other subatomic particles have been found.

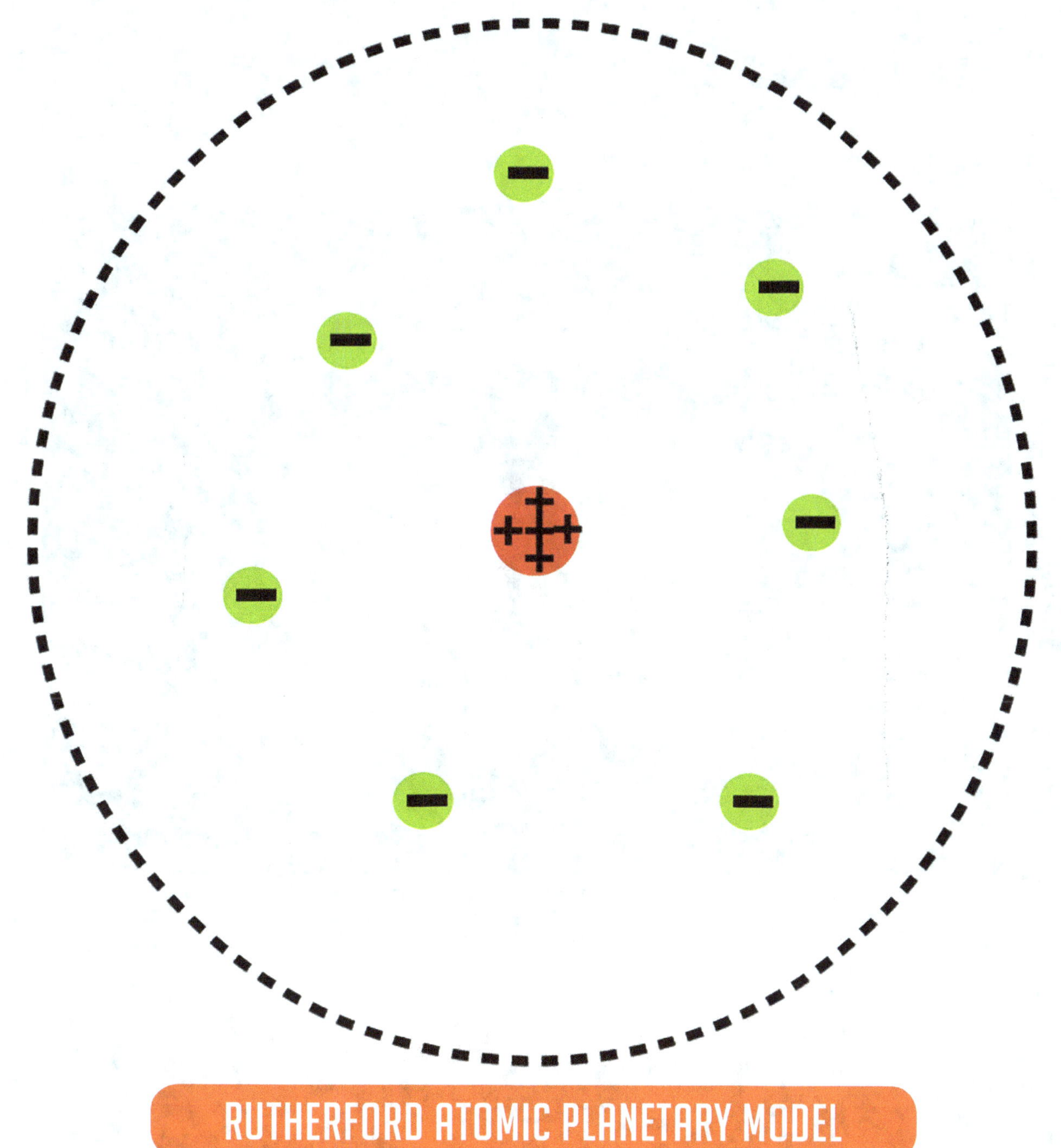

RUTHERFORD ATOMIC PLANETARY MODEL

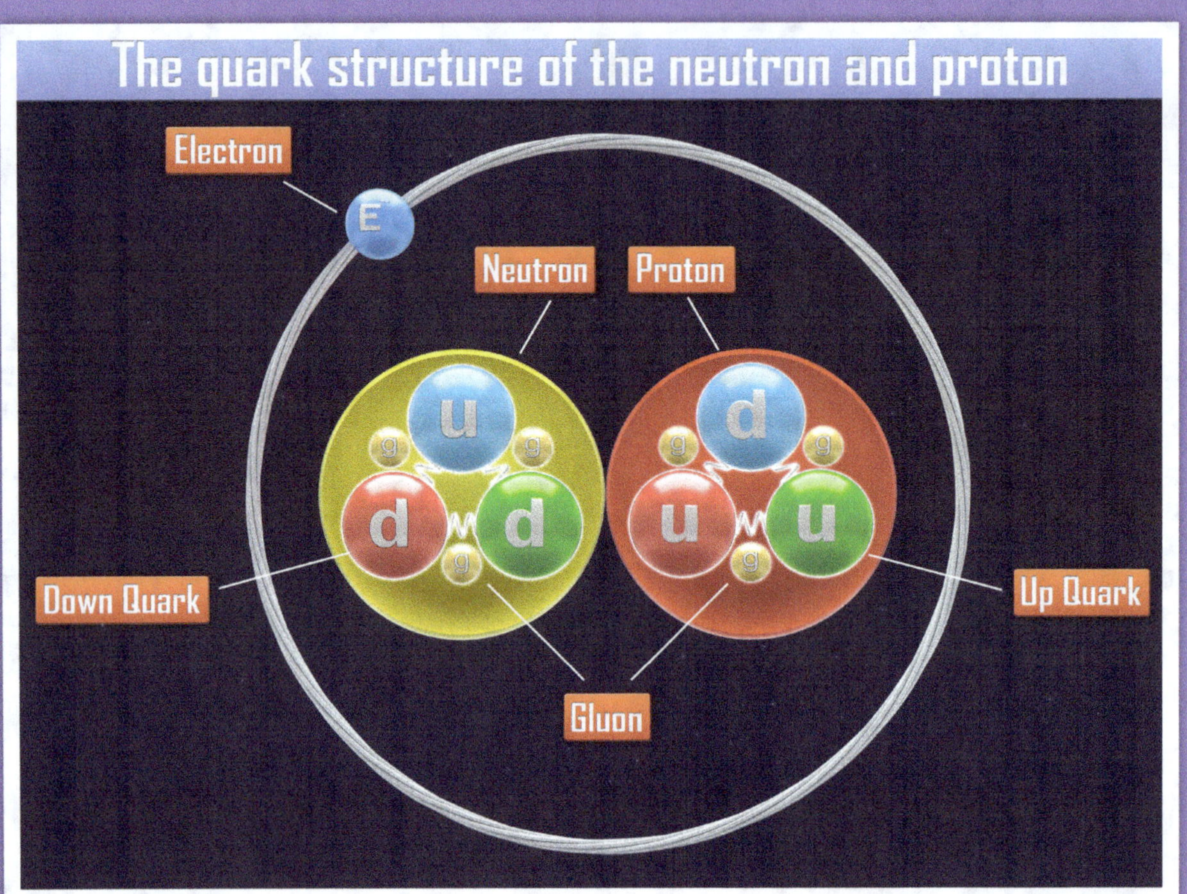

THE QUARK STRUCTURE OF
THE NEUTRON AND PROTON

In 1964, two scientists, Murray Gell-Mann and George Zweig, theorized that there were quarks. At that point in time, no one had observed evidence of quarks and they were known just from math calculations. They were found a few years later.

In 2012, another elementary particle was discovered. It had been theorized by physicist Peter Higgs fifty years before. This particle, called the Higgs boson, gives other particles their mass.

THE BASIC STRUCTURE OF THE ATOM

The basic parts of every atom are electrons, protons, and neutrons. There are 92 elements on Earth that exist through natural processes. For example, oxygen and sodium are both natural elements. They are made up of atoms that have different numbers of electrons, protons, and neutrons.

BOY BREATHING FRESH AIR IN NATURE

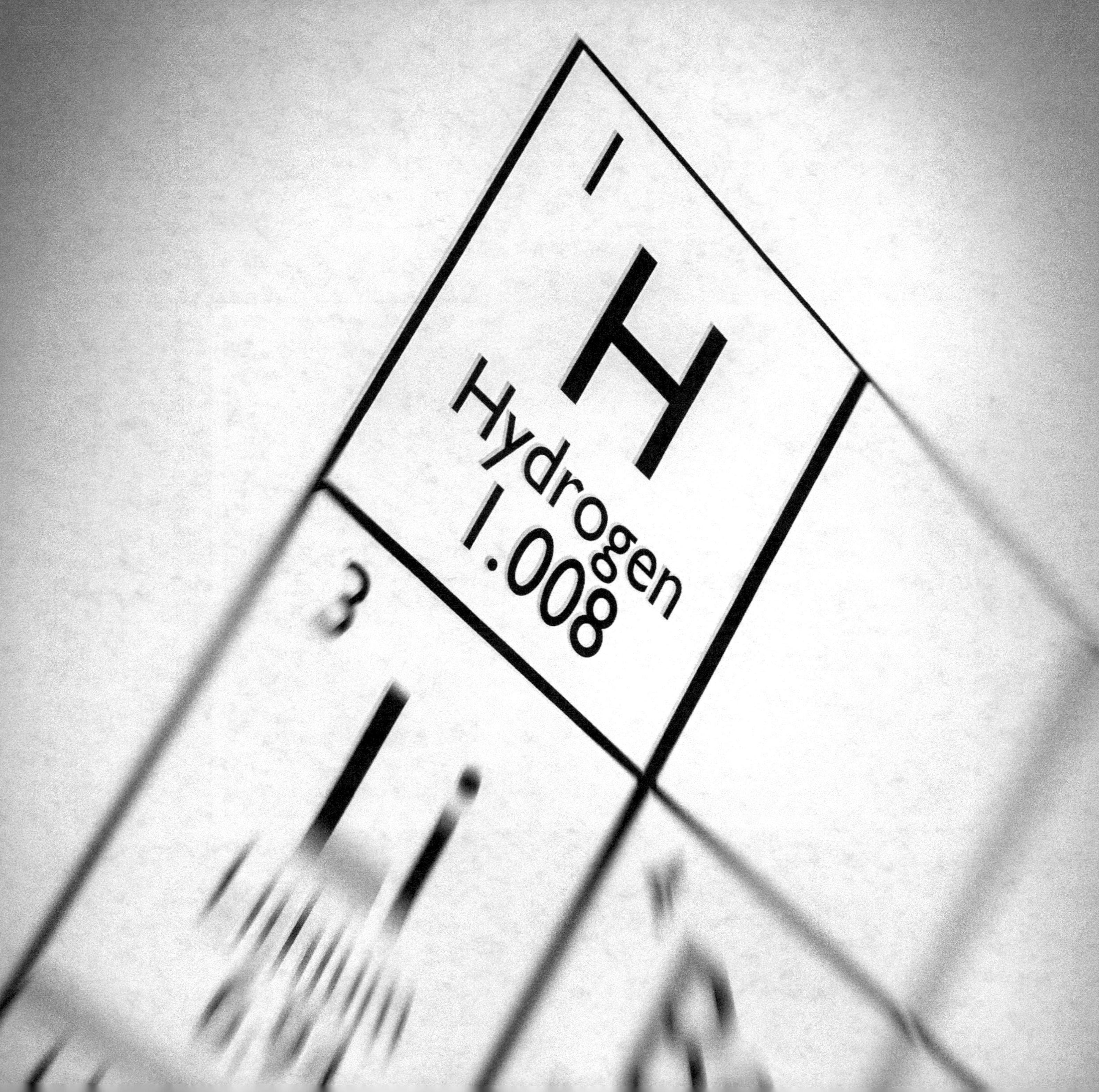

1
H
Hydrogen
1.008
3
Li

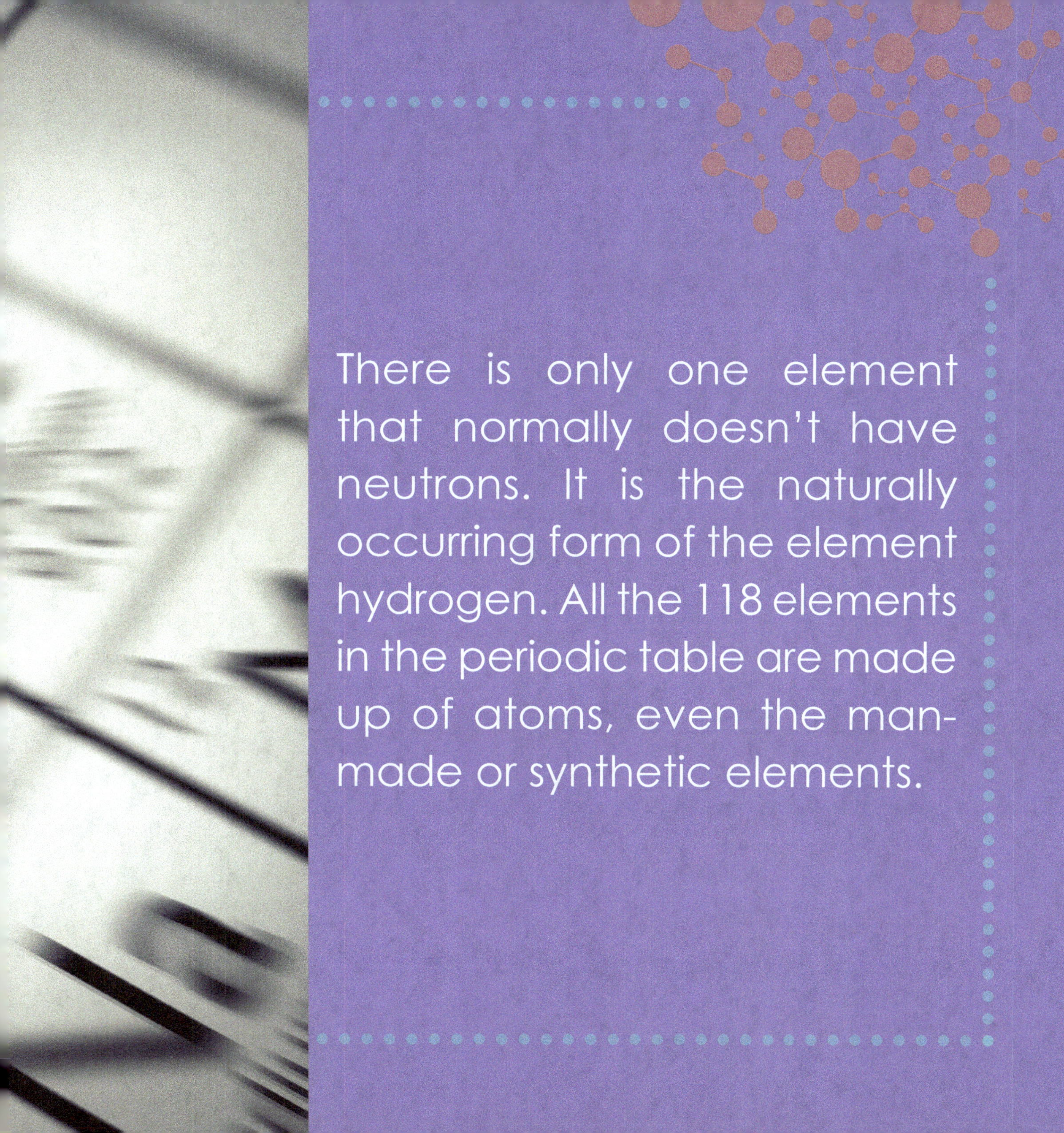

There is only one element that normally doesn't have neutrons. It is the naturally occurring form of the element hydrogen. All the 118 elements in the periodic table are made up of atoms, even the man-made or synthetic elements.

When chemicals react with each other, atoms from two or more different elements combine to make new compounds. For example, hydrogen and oxygen atoms combine to form water.

Nucleus

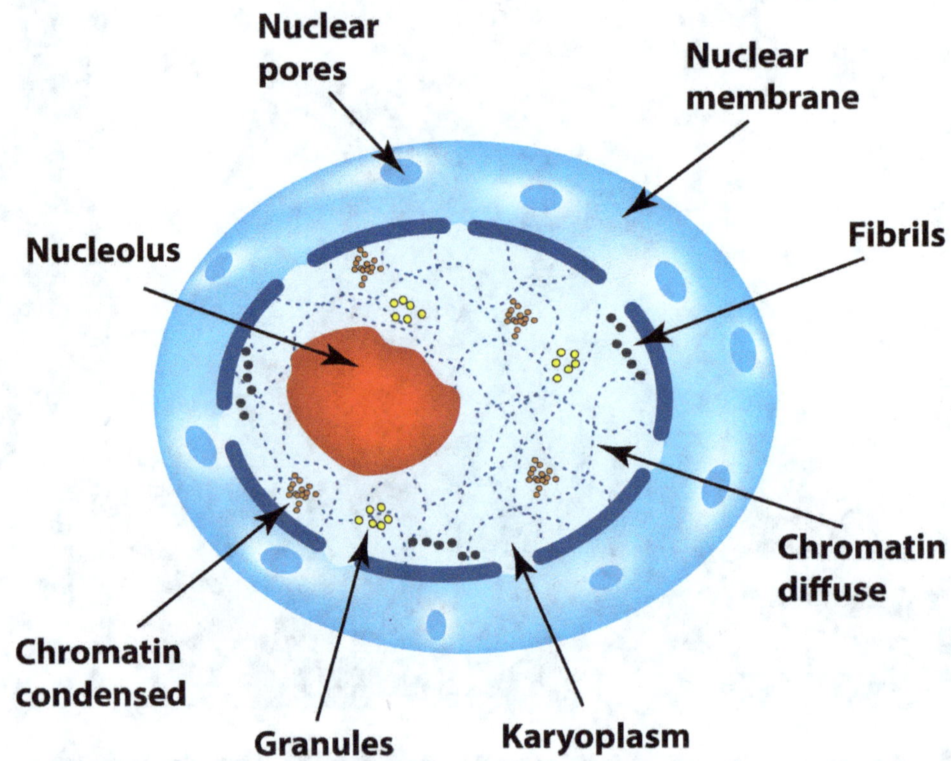

THE STRUCTURE OF THE HUMAN CELL NUCLEUS

The basic structure of the atom is deceptively simple. At its core are protons and neutrons. This central core of the atom is called its nucleus. The proton has a positive charge and the neutron has no charge. The quantity of neutrons in the atom of a specific element affects both its mass as well as its radioactivity.

The quantity of protons in an atom identifies what element that atom belongs to. For example, if an atom has 8 protons, then it is oxygen. If an atom has 80 protons, then it's the element mercury. In other words, each element has a unique quantity of protons and that number is its atomic number.

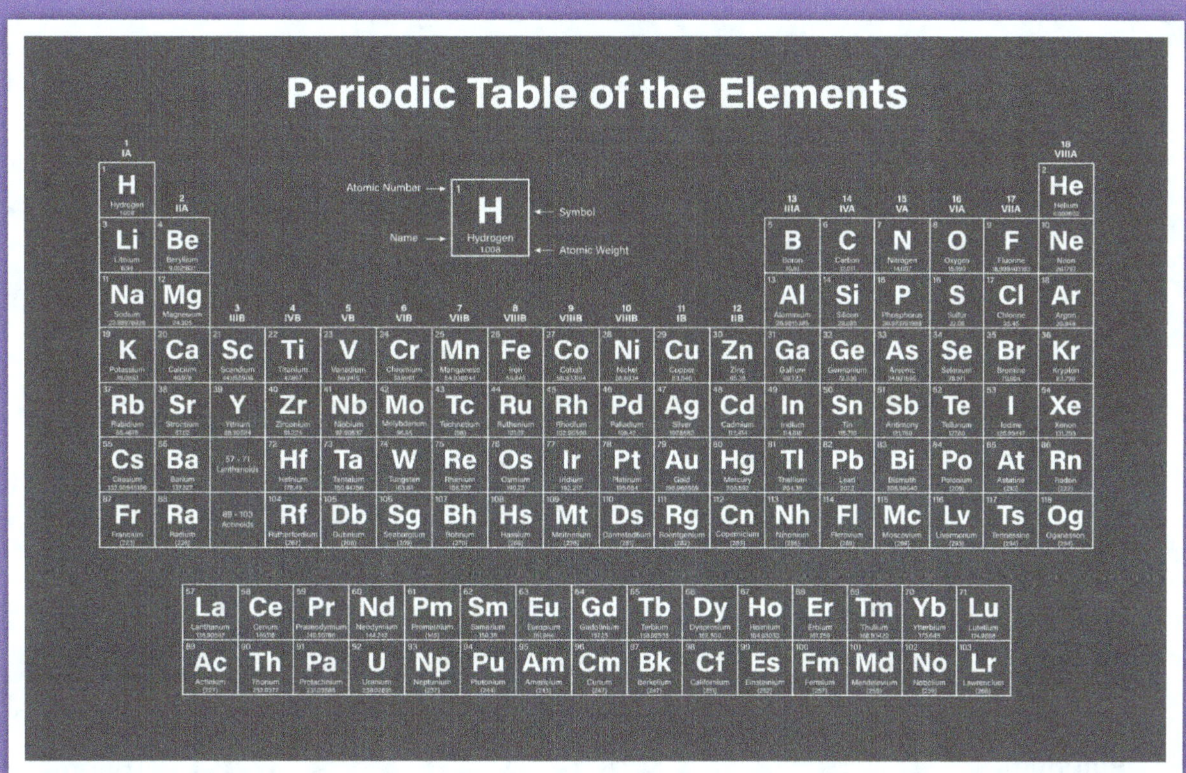

PERIODIC TABLE OF THE ELEMENTS

ISOTOPES OF HYDROGEN

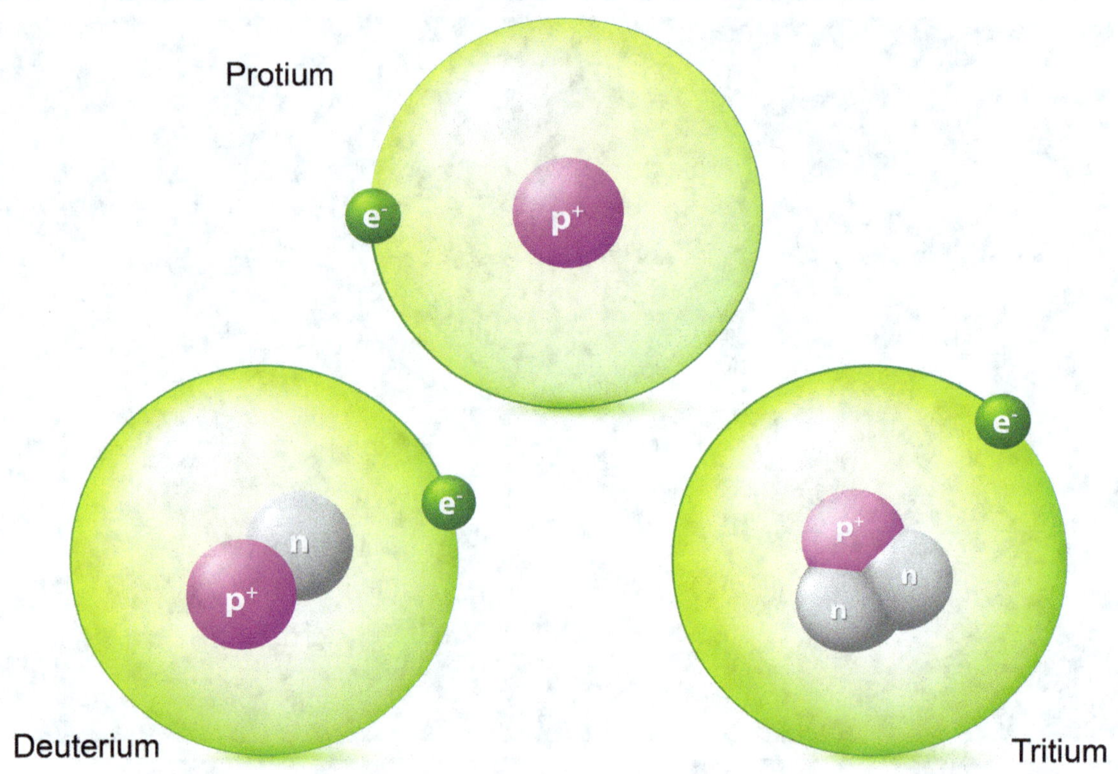

ISOTOPES OF HYDROGEN:
PROTIUM, DEUTERIUM AND TRITIUM

However, an atom can have different numbers of neutrons and still be an atom of the same element it was before. For example, the element of carbon always has 6 protons in its nucleus. Isotopes of the same element have different quantities of neutrons.

For example, carbon-12, carbon-13, and carbon-14 are all isotopes of carbon. Carbon-12 has 6 protons and 6 neutrons and it is a stable isotope. Carbon-13 has 6 protons and 7 neutrons and it is a stable isotope. However, carbon-14 has 6 protons and 8 neutrons and it is an unstable isotope.

RED CARBON DIOXIDE TANK

CARBON CYCLE

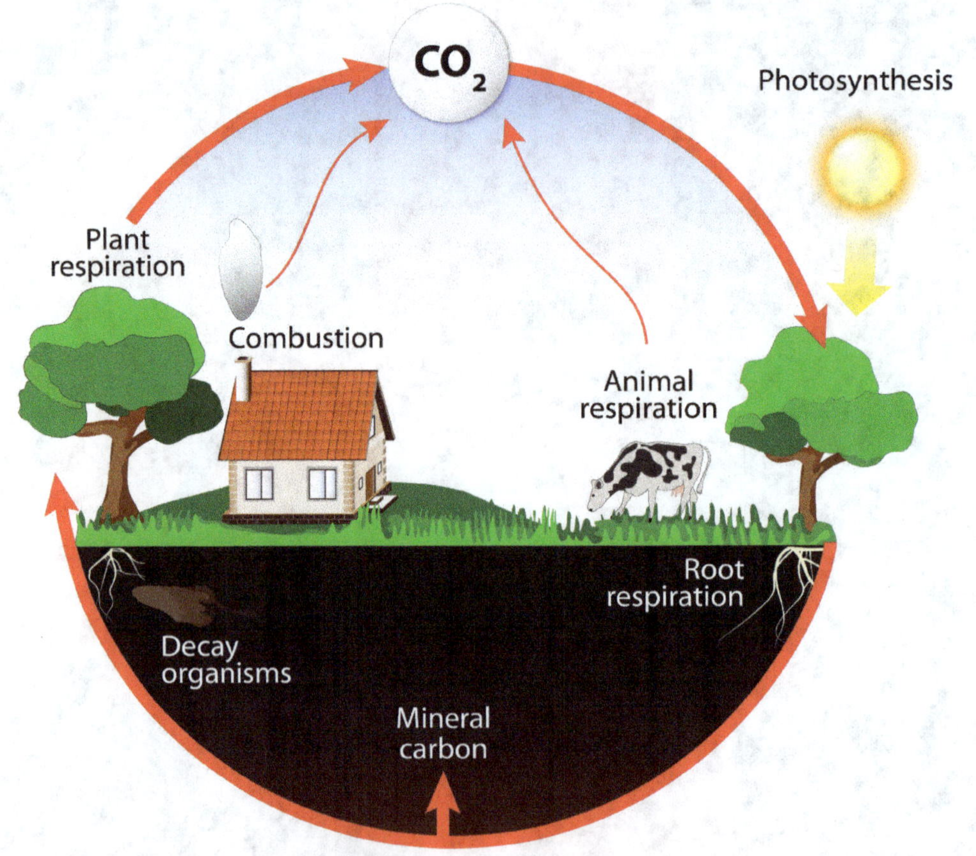

THE CARBON PATH FROM THE ATMOSPHERE, INTO LIVING ORGANISMS, THEN TURNING INTO DEAD ORGANIC MATTER, AND BACK INTO THE ATMOSPHERE.

Because of this additional neutron, the atom of carbon-14 has too much energy, and this makes it unstable. It will start releasing its excess energy, which means it is radioactive and will start to go through a process of decay.

The third basic part of the atom is the electron. Protons and neutrons are each much larger than electrons. A proton is about 1,800 times larger than an electron is. Electrons spin around the nucleus of an atom. They spin very fast so scientists can't predict exactly where they are located, but they can make estimates of where they should be.

GROUP OF SCIENTISTS WORKING AT
THE LABORATORY

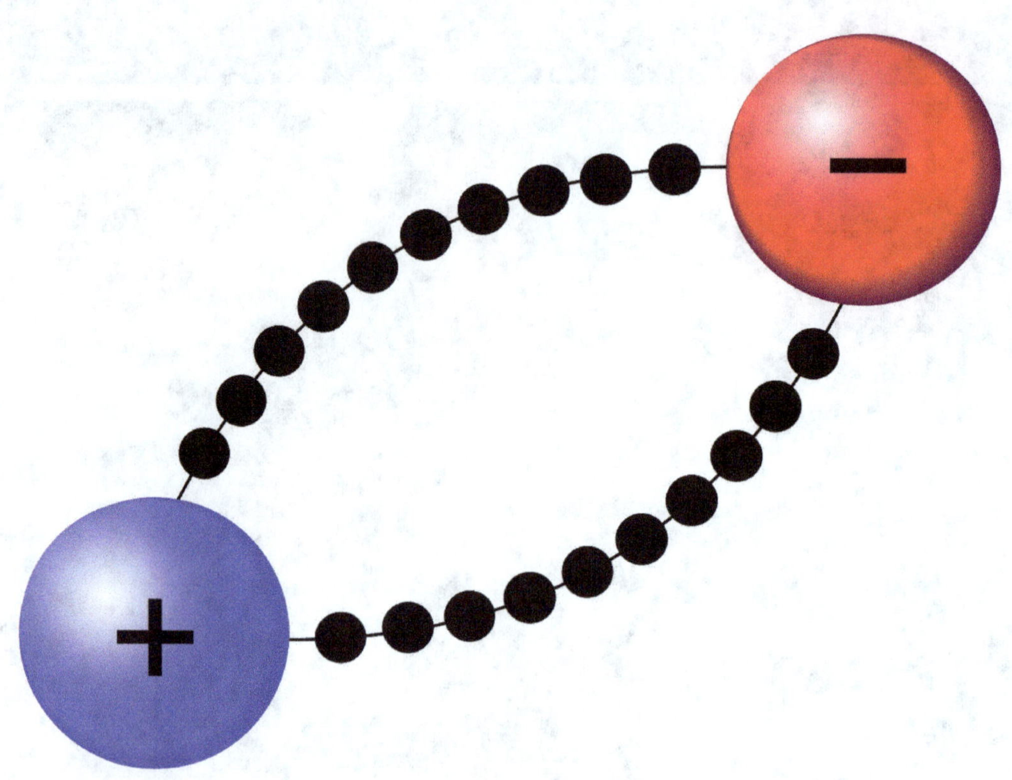

INTERACTION BETWEEN TWO OPPOSITELY CHARGED IONS (PARTICLES)

When an atom has the same number of protons and electrons, the positive and negative charges balance each other, out so the atom has a neutral charge. If it has more electrons than protons, it's negatively charged and when it has more protons than electrons, it's positively charged.

There is an amazing amount of energy locked up inside the nucleus of an atom. This power, which holds the protons and neutrons together is called the "strong force." An atom's nucleus can be split and the process for doing this is called nuclear fission.

NUCLEAR FISSION DEUTSCHES MUSEUM

NUCLEAR POWER PLANT

Nuclear power plants use the energy from the splitting of the atom to generate electricity. Unfortunately, the power from nuclear energy has also been used to create destructive bombs.

In summary, atoms have three basic parts:

- Elections that spin around the nucleus and have a negative charge
- Protons that are part of the atom's nucleus and have a positive charge
- Neutrons that are part of the atom's nucleus and have no charge

WHAT ARE ELEMENTARY PARTICLES?

An elementary particle is one that isn't made up of particles smaller than itself. At one time, philosophers and scientists thought that the atom was "uncuttable," but this has been shown not to be the case. As scientists are experimenting with atoms, more and more smaller particles have been found.

ELEMENTARY PARTICLES

STANDARD MODEL OF ELEMENTARY PARTICLES

DIAGRAM OF THE STANDARD MODEL OF PARTICLE PHYSICS.

Elementary particles are organized into two different categories. The first category is fermions. Fermions are the particles that create matter. There are two subcategories of fermions. Quarks are a subcategory of fermions and leptons are another subcategory of fermions.

The second category of elementary particles are bosons.

ALL MATTER IS MADE OF FERMIONS, WHICH ARE QUARKS AND LEPTONS

Quarks

Both protons and neutrons are made of quarks. Scientists have discovered six different types of quarks and have given them interesting names. Sometimes physicists refer to the different types as "flavors."

KIDS ANALYZING ATOMS

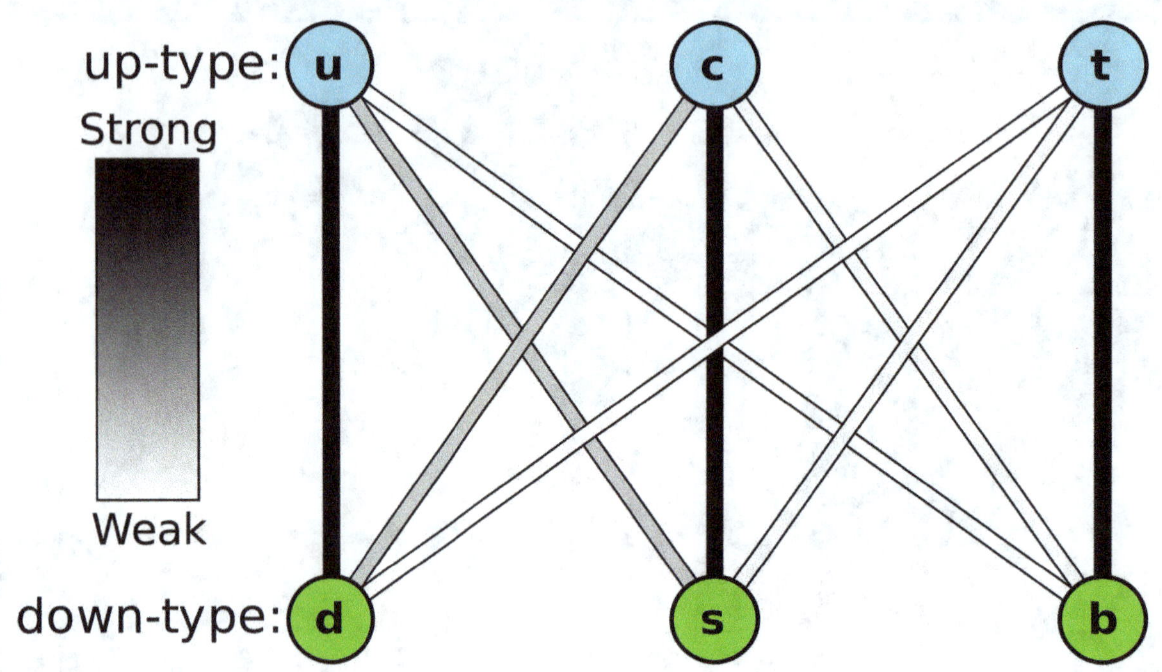

QUARK WEAK INTERACTIONS

The types of quarks are:

- up
- down
- top
- bottom
- charm
- strange

For example, a proton is composed of two "up" and one "down" quarks. A neutron, which balances with a proton, is made up of two "down" and one "up" quarks—the exact opposite configuration.

Leptons

So protons and neutrons are both made of different types of quarks. However, electrons are not made of quarks. At this time, physicists believe that electrons are elementary particles, however that's not known with 100% certainty and some scientists believe that they may be composed of smaller particles.

ATOM MODEL WITH QUARKS INSIDE PROTON
AND NEUTRON

WOMAN USING AN ELECTRON MICROSCOPE

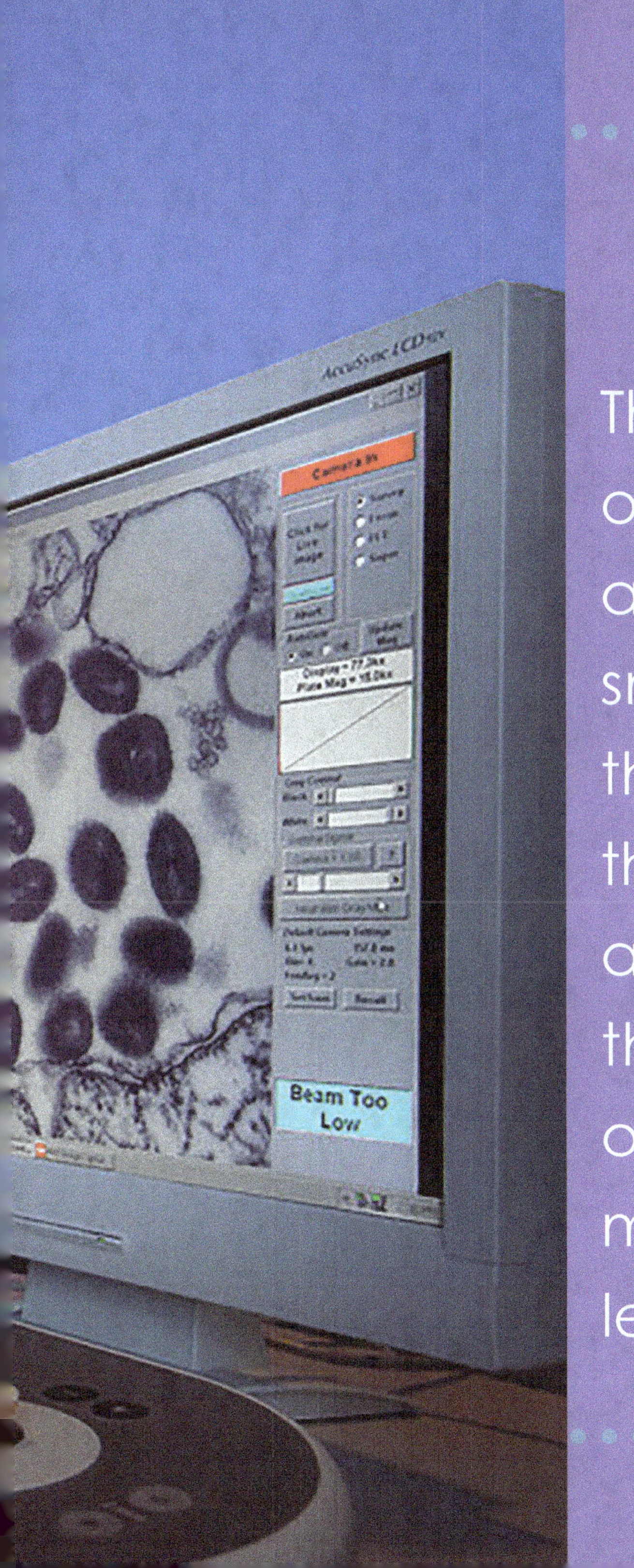

They fall into the category of leptons and it doesn't appear that they have smaller particles within them. The electron isn't the only type of lepton. In addition to the electron, there are other types of leptons, such as the muon lepton and the tau lepton.

Another type of lepton is a neutrino. Neutrinos are given off by the sun and pass right through solid matter, even our bodies! Nuclear reactions give off neutrinos as well. There are three types of neutrinos: electron neutrinos, muon neutrinos, and tau neutrinos.

In summary, the leptons are:

- electron
- muon
- tau
- electron neutrino
- muon neutrino
- tau neutrino

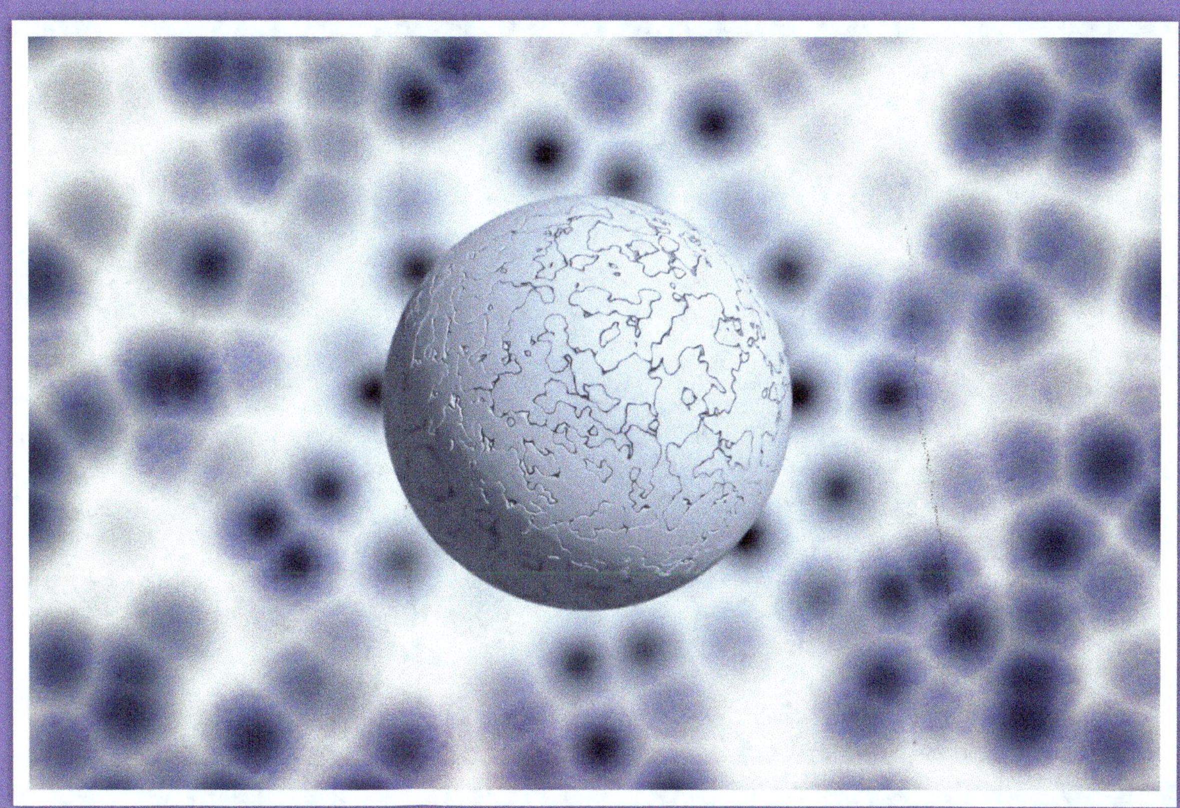

ISOLATED NEUTRINO

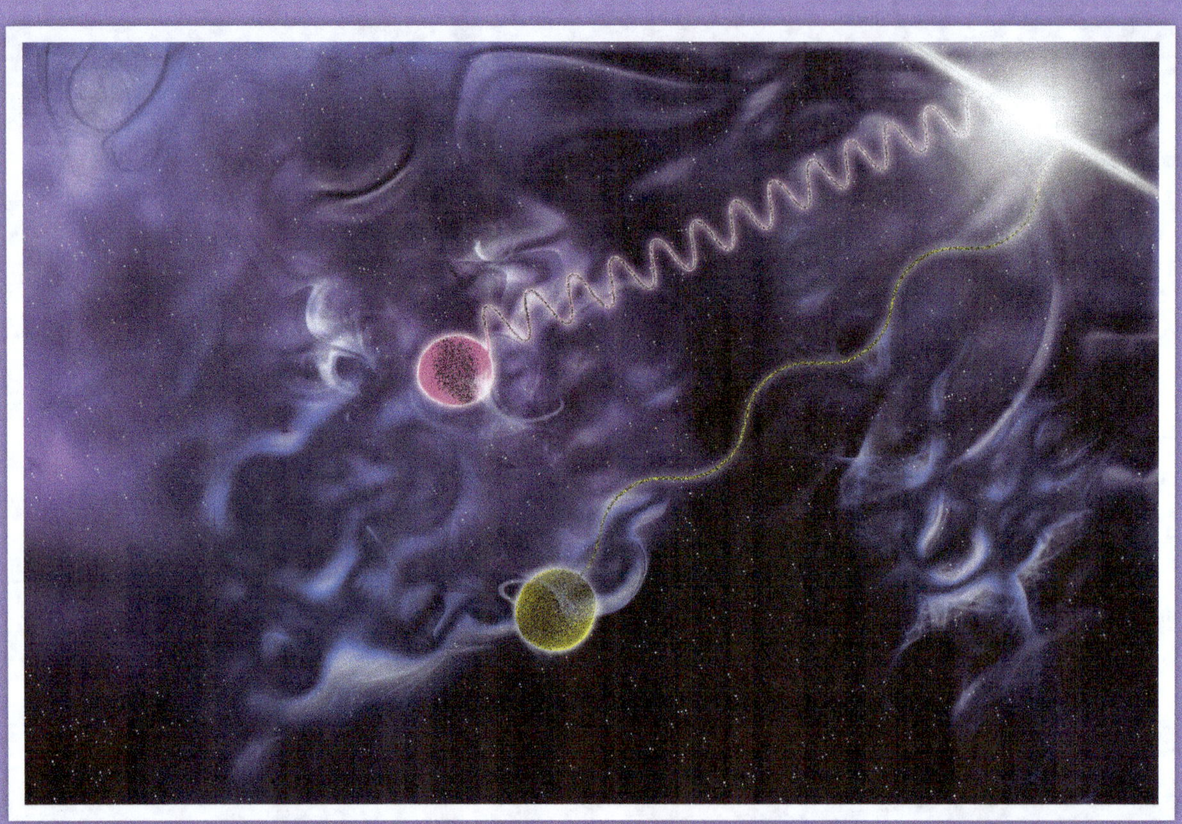

PHOTON

BOSONS CARRY FORCE

Just like fermions make up matter, bosons carry energy or force. For example, a photon, which is a type of particle that creates light, is a boson.

Another type of boson is the gluon. You can think of the gluon as the force that binds quarks together to create protons and neutrons. It is part of the "strong force" that holds the atom's nucleus together.

The Higgs boson was found in 2012. It has an influence on the mass of other particles.

Awesome! Now you know more about atoms and their subatomic parts. You can find more Physics books from Baby Professor by searching the website of your favorite book retailer.

www.ingramcontent.com/pod-product-compliance
Lightning Source LLC
Chambersburg PA
CBHW060614120726
48002CB00010B/2961